ROLES OF LOCAL GOVERNMENT IN RURAL DEVELOPMENT.

(Using Nigeria [West Africa] As A Case Study)

DIOGO SMART

© 2022 by Diogo Smart

Roles of Government in Rural Development

(Using Nigeria [West Africa] As A Case Study)

First Edition: May 2022

ISBN:

Published by:

Diadem Press Publishers.

<u>DEDICATION:</u>

This book is dedicated to everyone who is interested and optimistic for the smooth running of the government at the local level and for the development of urban areas.

Table of Contents

<u>INTRODUCTION</u>

The idea of local government administration in Nigeria has attracted serious attention both nationally and internationally since the local government reform of 1976. Agagu, (2007), viewed local government as a level of government which is supposed to have its greatest impact on the people at the rural areas. It is a tier of government which is closest to the citizenry and it is saddled with responsibility of guaranteeing the political, social and economic development of its area and its people (Enero, Oladoyin & Elumilade, 2009).

As a result of this development, there has been growing recognition of the importance of rural development as an instrument in the overall development of the contemporary developing world. This is because of the glaring gap between the rural and urban areas in terms of infrastructural, resources distribution, human resources development and employment, which has made rural development imperative (Ogbazi, 1982 in Zakari ya'u, 2014). This imbalance has subjected the rural areas to more disadvantaged economic position. It has induced rural – urban migration, thereby, increasing unemployment situation in the urban areas, while, simultaneously depriving the rural areas of their agricultural workforce (Zakari ya'u, 2014).

The idea of local government is to bring governance closer to people in the grassroots for participation in governance, service delivery to enhance socio-economic development and good governance (Ogunna, 2006 in Okoli, et al, 2015). But unfortunately, today, transparency and accountability in Nigerian local government is rhetoric, most local government officials display provocative wealth gotten through criminal institutionalized stealing and corrupt practices (Onah, 2010 in Okoli, et al, 2015).

The failure of local government in the area of service delivery over the years has made the citizens to lose faith and trust in local government administration as an institution in Nigeria.

From historical perspective, modern local government administration in Nigeria can be traced to the British system of local government. But it should be stated however, that local administration did not start with the advent of British Administration in Nigeria, because some forms of system of local government administration pre-dated the British rule. Local government administration is one of man's oldest institutions. The earliest form of local governments' administration existed in the form of clan and village meetings. In fact, democracy itself originated and developed along the lines of local governance initiative in the ancient Greek City States. It should be noted however, that in other parts of the world, local governance was developed along the people's culture and expectations, and the system was tied to the norms and practices of the people (Aghayere, 2007).

According to Gboyega, four points of historical reference can be identified in the development of local government administration in Nigeria. They are: (1) Colonial rule; (2) Local government reforms in the East (1951) and West (1952) respectively; (3) The military coup of 1966; and (4) The 1976 Local Government Reform (Gboyega as cited by Aghayere, 2007 in Oviasuyi et al, 2010).

Local government administration in Nigeria has undergone many changes of which the 1976

Reforms and the Constitutions of 1979 and 1999 can be said to be most prominent. Before 1976, local government administration in Nigeria had passed through many changing environments and this has in no small measure influenced its development. Again, the

1976 Local Government Reforms brought watershed in local government system; the reform brings unified structure and makes local government bedrock for development in the rural area (Agagu, 2009; Ajayi, 2005).

The reform was a major departure from the previous practice of local government administration in Nigeria. The philosophical basis of the reform lies in the conviction that a strong local authority with clearly defined functional responsibilities in a power-sharing relationship with the states is an institutional safeguard against tyranny. Following the 1976 reforms, local government became recognized as a tier of government entitled to a share of national revenue consequent on its constitutionally allocated functions (Imuetinyan 2007 in Oviasuyi et al, 2010)

The provisions of the 1976 reform document were incorporated into the 1979 Constitution of the Federal Republic of Nigeria. Section 7(1) of the constitution provides that "the government of every state shall ensure their existence under a law which provides for the establishment, structure, composition, finance and functions of such councils" Constitution of the Federal Republic of Nigeria (1979).

he power of the state government over local authorities has been rrongly applied to undermine elected and participatory governance nd responsibility at the grassroots, and this has made operation of he constitution questionable. The situation of local government dministration under the 1999 Constitution is also very confusing nd complex. Although, the 1999 Constitution also guarantees the xistence of a democratically elected local government system, it lowever, like the 1979 Constitution, gives the states the esponsibility to handle issues of organization and structure Oviasuyi et al, 2010).

ls a result of this development, most of the rural areas in Nigeria re in a pathetic state of development, even, some of the urban ocal government areas are also deficient in development. Some of hese infrastructures where available, are left uncared for. The mplication of this is that local governments in Nigeria have been consistent over the years in their failure to enhance their capacity to ngage and mobilize human resources towards their needs. Local oads are left unrepaired, rural electricity are in state of dilemma, ural health centres are dilapidated with absence of drugs and necessary health personnel, rural boreholes and water pumps have no water, rural water scheme/projects are deserted (Tolu, 2014).

CONCEPT OF LOCAL GOVERNMENT

The concept of local government involves a philosophical commitment to democratic participation in the governing process at the grassroots level. This implies legal and administrative decentralization of authority, power and personnel by a higher level of government to a community with a will of its own, performing specific functions as within the wider national framework. A local government is a government at the grassroots level of administration meant for meeting peculiar grassroots need of the people (Agagu, 2012). It is defined as "government by the popularly elected bodies charged with administrative and executive duties in matters concerning the inhabitants of a particular district or place (Appadorai, 2010).

Local government can also be defined as that tier of government closest to the people, "which is vested with certain powers to exercise control over the affairs of people in its domain" (Lawal, 2010). Akpan (2012) defined local government as "the breaking down of a country into smaller units or localities for the purpose of administration in which the inhabitants of the different units or ocalities concerned play a direct and full role through their elected representatives who exercise power and undertake functions under the general authority of the national or state government".

Barber (2014) defined Local government as authority to determine and execute matters within a restricted area. It becomes clear from the above that the purpose of establishing a local government is to ensure appropriate services and development activities responsible to local wishes and initiatives. Local government operates at the lowest level of society.

A local government is expected to play the role of promoting the democratic ideals of a society and coordinating development programme at the local level. It is also expected to serve as the basis of socio-economic development in the locality.

Ezeani (2014) favors the approach by Adamolekun (2012) in discussing local government within the purview of decentralization. Decentralization is typologised into "deconcentration" meaning administrative decentralization or field administration and "devolution" implying democratic decentralization in which there is substantial autonomy to sub-national units (i.e., local governments) with powers and responsibilities to perform specific functions given under the law by the central government. Duru (2013) converges with Ezeani (2014) and Adamolekun (2012) on the above approach and conceptualization of local government as devolution.

Proceeding from the above, Ezeani (2014) identified the following characteristics of devolution: local government must be granted autonomy and independence and be clearly recognized as a tier of government with little or no direct control by the central government. Local units must have clear and legally recognized geographical boundaries. Local governments must possess corporate status including the power to raise sufficient revenue to perform assigned functions. Devolution involves the need to "develop local governments as institutions". It also entails reciprocal, mutually benefiting and coordinate relationships between central and local governments.

An analysis of the above definitions reveals certain essential characteristics of local governments.

These are:

a. **Local Area:** A local government has to operate in a geographical area

b. **Statutory Status:** The local government enjoys statutory status i.e.; it is created by a specific law or statute.

c. **Autonomous Status:** Autonomy of the local governments is the natural consequence of their statutory status. Since the local governments are created by an act of the legislature, that Act lays down their powers, functions and relationship with central or state government.

d. **Local Participation:** Participation of the local people in decision making and administration of the local authority is important that is what gives it the character of self – government.

e. **Local Accountability:** Since local government provides services of local nature called civil amenities like sanitation, education, transport etc. to the people of the area, it is appropriate that it is accountable to the local people.

f. **Local Finances:** Local governments have two main sources of finances: (1) grants–in–aid given by the central or state government and (2) taxes and levies imposed by the local governments themselves.

g. **Social Services for the Local People:** The main objective of the local government is to provide certain civic amenities to the people of its area at their door – step. The provision of these services ensures healthy living of local community.

h. **Development:** In order to have a clearer picture of rural development, we need to understand the concept of development. Hornby (2010) defines development as the gradual growth of something so that it becomes more advanced, stronger, etc., the process of producing or creating something new. This definition implies that development involves a gradual or advancement through progressive changes. Umehali (2011) sees the changes to be multi-dimensional involving changes in structures, attitude and institutions as well as the acceleration of economic growth, the reduction of inequality and eradication of absolute poverty. He asserts that development involves economic growth component, equality or social justice component, and socio-economic transformational component which are all on a self-sustaining basis. Viewing the concept differently, Simon (2009) sees development as an improvement in quality of life (not just material standard of living) in both quantitative terms.

EVOLUTION OF LOCAL GOVERNMENT IN NIGERIA

Local government is a creation of British colonial rule in Nigeria. It has, over time, experienced change in name, structure and composition (Arowolo, 2010). Between 1930s and 940s, local government was known as Chief in Council, where raditional rulers were given pride of place in the scheme of things. n the 1950s, election was introduced according to the British nodel in the Western and Eastern parts of the country with some neasure of autonomy in personnel, financial and general .dministration (Nwabueze, 2002).

t was on this premise that the rising tide of progress, growth and levelopment experienced in the local governments in these areas vas based. The pace of this development was more noticeable in he South than in the North. During this period, heterogeneity was he hallmark of the local government as there was no uniformity in he system and the level of development was also remarkably lifferent.

The introduction of 1976 reforms by the military administration of General Obasanjo brought about uniformity in the administrative structure of the system; the reforms introduced a multi-purpose single-tier local government system (Ajayi, 2010). The reforms also introduced population criticism under which a local government could be created. Consequently, a population of within 150,000 to 800,000 was considered feasible for a local government (1976 Guidelines). This was done to avoid the creation of non-viable local council and for easy accessibility. There was provision for elective positions, having the Chairman as executive head of local government with supervisory councilors constituting the cabinet. This was complemented by the bureaucrats and professionals, who were charged with the responsibility of implementing policies.

In 1991, a major landmark reform was introduced as the system had legislative arm. In addition, the Babangida administration increased the number of local governments from 301 in 1986 to 453 in 1989 and 589 in 1991. The Abacha regime increased the number to 774 local councils that we presently have in Nigeria (Ajayi, 2000 in Tolu, 2014).

The precursor of local government was the native administration established by the colonial administration. As one of its principal uthors posited, Native Administration was: Designed to adapt to purposes of local government the tribal institutions which the native people have evolved for themselves so that the latter may develop in a constitutional manner from their own past, guided and restrained by the traditions and sanctions which they have inherited, molded or modified as they may be on the advice of the British officers. It is an essential feature of the system, within the limitations, the British Government rules through these native institutions which are regarded as an integral part of the machinery of Government with well-defined powers and functions recognized by Government and by law and not dependent on the caprice of an executive officer (Cameron 1964).

The Native Administration was charged with the collection of taxes, maintenance of law and order, road construction and maintenance, and sanitary inspection, especially in township areas. This system of government, which was modelled after the Millsian ideal of local representation, generated two types of conflicts among the fledging ethnic groups in Nigeria.

The first arose in cases where two or more ethnic groups were 'lumped together' in one native administration. Given what Post and Vickers (1993) have aptly called the 'differential incorporation' of Nigerian peoples into Nigeria, some groups who had earlier access to the British and had acquired some education tended to dominate the Native Administration. If such domination could be justified, as the British did, on the grounds of the opportunity it afforded the privileged group to groom others in the art of governance, the superimposition of the paramount ruler of one group as permanent native authority even when there was no pre-colonial history of dependent relations, encouraged local separatism. Most of the groups joined in such non-consensual matrimony agitated for separation and independence.

As Igbuzor, (2010), noted "in 1976, the federal government embarked in collaboration with the state government embarked on extensive reform on which were outlined as follows: -

a) To make appropriate services and development activities responsive to local wishes and initiatives by devolving or delegating them to local representative bodies.

b) To facilitate the exercise of democracy self-government close to the Grass root of our society.

c) Mobilization of human and materials through the involvement of members of the public in their local government.

1) To provide a two-way channel of communication between local government (both state and federal)

For the first time in history of local government in Nigeria a uniform system was developed for the whole country. According to the then chief of staff, supreme headquarters, Brigadiers Shehu Yardua in his forward to the reform stated thus, "Was essentially motivated by the necessity to stabilize and nationalize government at the local level.

Unlike the previous reform measures which were restricted in scope and range. The 1976 local government reform conceptualized local government as the third tier of government operating within common institutional framework. The intentions of 1976 reforms were debated by the Constitution Drafting Committee (CDC) and the constituent assembly in 1978 and were enshrined in the 1979 constitutions. The Dasuki reform of 1984 and 1988 reform further consolidated the position of local government in the country. Hence, they have all been in corporate in the constitution of the federal republic of Nigeria 1999. The reform went further to enshrine the principle of participatory democracy and of political responsibility to every Nigerian.

In summary, it can be said that no public institution in Nigeria has been so subjected to frequent reforms than local government. Nearly every successive administration introduces one administrative change or the other. Apart from the celebrated 1976 reforms, state government officials have also introduced various manipulations.

THE AREAS IN WHICH THE LOCAL GOVERNMENT CAN FACILITATE RURAL DEVELOPMENT:

a. **Economic Sector:** The bulk of the population live in the rural areas hence; every economic development measure should take special note of rural dwellers and their problems. Therefore, local governments should be involved in economic planning and execution both of the federal and the state government. That way, they stand a better chance of mobilizing their people to support government policies alleviation measures as well as create jobs for their teeming population. By so doing, they improve their economy and address the problem of poverty.

Health Sector: The state of health centers in most local government is to say the least deplorable. There is abject nonexistence of drugs, medical equipment and manpower. Again, there is increasing lack of enthusiasm among health personnel as a result of which most inhabitants of the rural areas resort to traditional medical practices. Some has fallen victims to fake drugs sold by most local dispensaries and medicine shops.

Indeed, local government stands a better chance of tackling the health problems of the rural people by addressing the problems bedeviling the sector.

Transportation and Communication: Local government should construct and maintain local roads and by so doing ease the burden of transportation hanging on the neck of the inhabitants of rural areas. Also, they can set up mass transit as a way of checking the skyrocketing cost of transportation. In the area of communication, efforts should be geared towards encouraging Global Service Mobile (GSM) services providers to connect the nook and crannies of their localities.

d. **Provision of Essential Amenities:** Such basic social amenitie as good roads, network, electricity, water and recreationa facilities are very much lacking in the rural communities acros the country. Therefore, the local government should partne with the central and state government in providing them. By s doing the problem of rural urban drift will be checked.

e. **Agricultural sector:** Notwithstanding the craze for oi agriculture remains the mainstay of the country's economy Majority of Nigerian depend on agriculture, especially the rura dwellers, to generate income. In Nigeria, mechanization of th sector remains at a low ebb. Government can and should com to the help of the farmers by way of providing them with sof loans, subsidized farm inputs such as fertilizer, improve seedlings, insecticides and even farm implements for planting operations. Also, seminars and workshop should be organize during which farmers are taught best agricultural practices.

f. **General Security:** Security of lives and properties remain indispensable in every developmental planning and programmes. Resources are made and kept or reinvested fo greater results or dividends. Hence, therefore, efforts should be geared towards ensuring reasonable peace and mutual coexistence between local communities. Such atmosphere promotes programme and project execution and resources collection.

g. **Industrialization:** Local government can contribute to rural development through rural industrialization by setting up cottage industries such as garri processing plants, rice milling centers, palm-oil processing units, fishing and livestock outfits etc. Such ventures provide employment to the people and empower them financially. Other ways in which rural development can be attained is by encouraging community projects such as road construction, rural electrification, water projects and so on. Also, local government can address the perennial housing problems facing Nigerians by embarking on housing projects.

h. **Education Sector:** Education is an indispensable index of development. Though aware of the importance of education in any planned natural development, not much has been done by successive administrations to provide functional qualitative education to Nigerians especially the rural dwellers. Against the backdrop of the important consequences therefore, we expect local government to redouble their efforts in this regard. Not only should schools be built but of important is the need to promote the quality of teaching staff in the schools through training and improved welfare packages. Again, relevant teaching and learning aids such as textbooks, classrooms, office accommodation and furniture should be provided (Agboh & Attansey, 2014).

i. **Encouraging Communal Self-help Projects:** In this case, the government at the grass root level should in one way or the other encourage different communities to form an organization or group that will work towards enhancing the rural development in their different villages/communities. This is because; the government cannot tackle the whole problems at a time.

PROBLEMS OF LOCAL GOVERNMENT IN NIGERIA

a. A Local Government is an administrative unit with a defined territory, administration authority, power and relative autonomy. It is governed by either selected or elected members from the community. Most countries of the world are apparently committed to establishing Local Governments irrespective of the fact that there is no consensus on whether they should exist or not (Bello-Iman, 2006). The problems of Local Governments in Nigeria can only be examined in relation to the objectives upon which its creation in Nigeria was predicated.

b. The four basic purposes for the establishment of Local Government according to the Local Government Reforms Guidelines (1976) include; enhancement of participatory democracy, promotion of local freedom of action or local autonomy, political integration and national unity, and the provision of services for which they are the most efficient providers compared to other levels of government. It is therefore, obvious from the literature that a number of factors inhibit the actualization of these objectives. The poor performance of Local Government as a tool for promoting rural development and participatory democracy at the grassroots has been constrained by a wide range of factors.

c. The most notorious of the constraints, according to Bello-Imam (2006) and Enemuo (2009), is inadequate finance. The problem arises from their inability to source for revenue internally coupled with insufficient allocation from the central government. This raped them of their functions as they hardly have the finance to execute meaningful rural development projects. Inadequate skilled and experienced personnel are yet another problem. This Ameh (2008) calls Lack of resources, Local Government lack skilled manpower to facilitate a high rate of service delivery. Sorkaa (2009), states that, the era of party politics affects immensely the recruitment, discipline and condition of service of Local Government staff and hence the performance of Local Governments in Nigeria.

d. Another problem is the excessive interference and control by the central government. This undermines local autonomy of the third tier of government. In Nigeria, the federal and state governments have mostly led the dissolution of elected Local

Governments chairmen and councilors before the expiration of their tenure. Bello-Imam (2006) opines that the intergovernmental relationship between Local Governments and the higher levels of government witnessed suffocating controls and sometimes conflicting directives. This causes a lot of problem to the local level and the performance of Local Governments in general. Corruption, lack of political will and honesty constitutes another serious problem to Local Government performance in Nigeria. Ameh (2008) asserts that, corruption at this level of government covers aspects like embezzlement of finds, falsification of receipts and accounts, inflation of figures on payment vouchers, inflation of prices of goods and services rendered and unnecessary employment of staff.

Sorka agrees with the above when he says that, corruption and unethical behavior has eaten deep into the fabric of the Local Government system of Nigeria. He further opines that most top functionaries of Local Government are not always objective; administrative work is personalized, rules are not taken seriously and sometimes, even discarded completely (Sorkaa, 2006; 2009).

f. The above implies high incidence of corrupt use of office, lack of integrity and unlawful appropriation of public funds particularly internally generated revenue for personal gains. This is what the higher level of government used as an excuse for the controlled autonomy of Local Governments.

g. There is also the problem of inadequate support in some quarters. This stems from the poor performance of Local Government in rural development and service delivery at the grassroots. In the recent past many scholars and even top government officers have called for scrapping of Local Governments in Nigeria. This according to Denga (2008) was as a result of their poor performance of their traditional role in the recent past.

CONCEPT OF RURAL DEVELOPMENT

a. An understanding of the concept of development will give a clearer picture of rural development. Hornby (2010) defines development as the gradual growth of something so that it becomes more advanced, stronger, etc.; the process of producing or creating something new. This definition implies that development involves a gradual or advancement through progressive changes. Umebali (2011) sees the changes to be multi-dimensional involving changes in structures, attitude and institutions as well as the acceleration of economic growth; the reduction of inequality and eradication of absolute poverty. He asserted that development involves economic growth components, equality or social justice's component and socio-economic transformational components which are all on a self-sustaining basis.

b. Simon (2009) sees development as an improvement in quality of life (not just material standard of living) in both quantitative terms. He opines that development must be seen as actually and temporally relative, needing to be appropriate to time, space, society, culture. Rural Development simply connotes a sustained improvement in the quality of life of the rural people. It implies consistency in approach in which micro and macro-economic, social political, cultural and technological variables are engineered, combined and implemented as an organic and dynamic whole for the benefit of the people (Onurah 2011). Rural development is sometimes used synonymously with agricultural development efforts. It is on this account that the nitrated rural development projects in Nigeria were designed to ensure that agricultural and rural development efforts become part of package of services offered to farmers and the rural population (Ijere and Mbanasor, 2010).

c. The bottom line really is poverty alleviation consequent upon increase in rural productivity, income and diversification of rural economic, improvement in the supply of rural infrastructure (physical, social and institutional), enhancement of social participant and radical improvement of the quality of life of the rural people. The concept of rural development has been broadened in recent time to accommodate non-economic issues, this broadened rural development concept, otherwise known as the sustained rural development, takes a long-term view of which meets the needs of the present generation without compromising the needs of future generation (Michener, 2008).

d. The concept of rural development in Nigeria lacks a unified definition as different scholars tend to view it from varying perspectives. Some scholars look at rural development from the aspect of education/training like (Haddad, 2000 and Hinzen,

2007). Obinne (2011) perceived rural development to involve creating and widening opportunities for (rural) individuals to realize full potential through education and share in decision and action which affect their lives. He viewed effort to increase rural output and create employment opportunities and root out fundamental (or extreme) cases of poverty, diseases and ignorance. Others like Olayide, Ogunfowora, Essang and Idachaba (2011) view rural development as means for the provision of basic amenities, infrastructure, improved agriculture productivity and extension services and employment generation for rural dwellers.

From the foregoing, it is obvious that rural development is not a one-off thing or an immediate and snap phenomenon. Rather, it is a gradual and progressive towards perfection having a set standard in mind. Rural development has variously been defined; Olayide et al (2011) see rural development as a process whereby concerted efforts are made in order to facilitate significant increase in rural resources productivity with the central objective of enhancing rural income and creating employment opportunity in rural communities for rural dwellers to remain in the area. It is also an integrated approach to food production, provision of physical, social and institutional infrastructures with an ultimate goal of bringing about good healthcare delivery system, affordable and quality education, improved and sustainable agriculture etc. As it is today, rural development needs to be given priority attention. Several reasons for such urgency include high and unacceptable rate of poverty, poor access to safe drinking water supply and sanitation, higher rate of health indicator such as infant mortality rate, malnutrition and diseases prevalence and lower enrolment of children in school.

THE ROLES OF LOCAL GOVERNMENT IN RURAL DEVELOPMENT

Local government development is a broad term covering the basic facilities and services needed for rural communities and rural development (FAO, 2011). It is designed as the totality of basic physical facilities upon which all other economic activities in a system depend (African Development Bank, 2009, Geet, 2012). Rural development comprises the assets needed to provide people with access to economic and social facilities and services such as roads, water, drainage, bridges, electricity etc. Local government is a government at the grassroots level of administration meant for meeting the peculiar needs of the rural people (Agagu, 2007). In his analysis, he viewed local government as a level of government which is supposed to have its greatest impact on the people at the rural areas. It is a tier of government which in physical terms is closest to the citizenry and it is saddled with responsibility of guaranteeing the political, social and economic development of its area and its people (Enero, Dadoyin and Elumilade, 2009).

Appadorai (1995) observed that there are problems that are local in nature and such problems are better handled by local government because they are better understood by the local people themselves. Based on the 1976 guidelines for local government reform, it is expected that local government should engage in rural infrastructural provision to engender development and good governance at the grassroots. But unfortunately, local government still lacks behind in the area of infrastructure, this ugly trend is particularly greater in the area of water and sanitation, rural road access and electricity.

According to World Bank (2009) Nigeria's infrastructure in terms of quality and quantity is grossly inadequate and inferior to that existing in other parts of the world. Out of the 102 countries assessed in the global competitiveness report in 2004, the Nigeria's quality of infrastructure was ranked 3rd to the last, this is consistent with the World Bank survey results where manufacturing firms listed infrastructure as their most severe business constraint. The Nigerian roads were described as the lowest in density in Africa, where only 31% of the roads are paved as compared to 50% in the middle-income countries, and even where roads are provided, only 40% of these roads can be said to be in good condition (Alabi and

Ocholi, 2010). Currently only 20% of Nigeria's rural population have access to electricity.

In Nigeria, it was observed in Amuro district in Kogi State that passengers pay 3 times for kilometer on untarred rural roads compared to tarred roads. A nation-wide survey was conducted by the Central Bank of Nigeria (CBN) on the state of roads in the country; the survey revealed that the road network, as at December 2002, was estimated at 194,000 kilometers, with the Federal Government being responsible for 17%, state government 16% and local government 67%. It was also shown that most of the roads were in bad condition, especially those in rural areas (CBN, 2010). Some of the roads constructed over 30 years ago had not been rehabilitated even once, resulting in major cracks and numerous potholes that make road unsafe. Water is critical to human existence but yet a serious problem of human survivals, health and economic development. Millions of people in developing countries are faced with acute water stress from inadequate supplies.

Survey conducted by Hall (2011) revealed insufficient or lack of provision of pipe borne or portable drinking water where 50% of the city dwellers and 90% of rural dwellers lack access, as a result, large proportion of households have resorted to drawing water from unhygienic sources. Most of the rural areas in Nigeria are in a pathetic state of infrastructure delivery, even, some of the urban local government areas are also deficient in infrastructure delivery. Some of these infrastructures where available, are left uncared for. The implication of this is that local governments in Nigeria have been consistent over the years in their failure to enhance their capacity to engage and mobilize the people and to respond to their needs and to administer effectively and responsibly the various local services needed for grassroots development. Local roads are left unrepaired, rural electricity are in state of dilemma, rural health Centre's are dilapidated with absence of drugs and necessary health personnel, rural boreholes and water pumps have no water, rural water scheme/projects are deserted. The only visible things in the rural areas are the sign post that shows the location, direction, and physical status of these rural infrastructures. So many of them are not functioning due to long years of existence, lack of maintenance, uncompleted nature of the projects, vandalization, lack of quality job and absence of community ownership of such projects (Tolu, 2014).

Communal effort has not been a recent phenomenon. It dates back to the time of primitive communalism when people searched for their living communally. In the early state of man, he always sought ways of conquering nature. Bryne (2003) argues that the concept of community development is not new, that rather it is an old ideology. The reality in Bentham's assertion that community development is a man in the society can be sustained by the fact that communities throughout history constructed and maintained their roads, bridges, square, sunk their well for good drinking water supply, and constructed their markets, village churches and village halls by community efforts.

Lawal, (2013) community development is not new in Nigeria, that what is actually new nowadays in community development are techniques and methods through which new pattern of leadership emerges from the rank and file.

Dare, (2009) in his own contribution argues that though local government is a veritable vehicle for community development, most local government have not made appreciate impact in this direction. He attributes the problem to the myriad of functions allocated to local government without commensurate financial backing.

Ogunna (2000) attributed the low performance of local government to the following factors; inadequate revenue, low executive capacity, poor and inadequate working materials, incompetence and ineptitude of existing staff and excessive control by the state government which result in delays and red-tapism. The solution, he suggested, lies in the review of the local government system particularly in areas of financial relationship with the state government and personnel. This control of local government was made clear in the implementation, guideline on the application of the civil service. Reform in the local government service.

Okunade, (2008) expressing his own idea, state that the spread of counties has provided the awareness among rural dwellers, and has provided the existence for a concept of the process of community development and of project which have been set in motion since the United National Organization development its concepts since thirty years ago. Community development draw greater inspiration from the desire for a change and in the ability of man to learn and charge through the voluntary method, (that is, free from coercion) and through the participation of individuals and groups in the development process for the achievement of some definite goals.

According to Sehinde, (2013) community development is: A process of education by which people of all ages and interest in the community, learn to share their thoughts, their ideas, the participation, their joys and their sorrows and in a large measure to mold and shape the communal destiny for themselves. It is a process of self-discovery by the time the people of a community learn to identify and solve their community problems.

A firm grasp at their beliefs and value system will throw light on what the community accepts as good and bad, as right or wrong. In turn, changes achieved by community effort can influence the beliefs and value system of a community. It is necessary to stimulate the self-help spirit of the people by mobilizing them for communal efforts, which should be sustained with the assistance of the government. Blue Print for rural development, argues that for effective implementation of strategies for community development the town and community unions, age grades, etc. should be linked with government. This idea he said is to involve the community people fully through their union, age grades and other similar policies that are designed to improve their economic, social, political and cultural development. He stated that this would enable them to make positive contributions to both rural and national development. The community union and age grade in every community have usually served as point of articulation and fully aware of the needs of the people. However, if they are fully integrated into the planning stage of development project, a lot will be achieved.

Writing on rural development in Nigeria, Mabogunje, (2002) in his book "leading issues in Nigerian Rural Development" accused successive Nigerian government at being previous regimes, rather than developing the rural areas. He contents that this is the general pattern all over the third world countries. Mabogunje, remarked that many strategies such as "authoritarian hand out" from the administration which prescribed the facilities suitable for the rural areas and two, the so-called development from below have been tried in the past, in the attempt to solve rural poverty in Nigeria. These strategies have however not proved successful; he looks at rural development problem such as lack of coordinated community development programmes, manpower problems of infrastructure problem of relevant rural education. He suggests solutions to these problems, which include clear understanding of the concept community development, an integrated development programmes, provision of infrastructure, relevance at rural education to the peculiar need and aspiration of the rural areas.

Local government and rural development in Nigeria, Olowo, et al., and (2011) describes government approach to rural development as a sham. According to him, government has succeeded in imposing development programme on the rural masses, such programme he argues, only benefited a few rich and powerful urban elite. He calls for a model of rural development, which involves the genuine participation of the rural people. Such he continues will be relatively independent of centralized urban-oriented bureaucratic machines.

Nwaka, (2009) on his part argued that government imposition of rural development programme on the communities have been Cog in the wheal of rural development. As he put it, government have often set community development; priorities without the participation of the target or relevant communities. He suggests that since government, communities are the engines of growth; government should play down its excessive control in betting out development goals and priorities for local communities.

Nnoli, (2000) sees self-help, as a strategy for rural development as a form of exploitation because, according to him, for the rural people it is viewed as the task resort to their survival due to government neglect. According to him, the community development process arises from the crying need of the rural population for social welfare services, unwillingness of the rural class to provide these amenities, the exploitation of the ruling class of the competition among communities for those social artifacts which are deemed to reflect social progress, and the exploitation by the ruling class at the tendency by Nigerians to invest more time, energy and resources and those tasks approved by their communities than those sanctioned by the national collectively via-the-state.

Okoli, (2005) in his book contends that the British colonialists in Nigeria hatched community development ideology in order to under develop the people through his negative manipulation strategy. He regrets that his strategy has continued to be employed by indigenous rulers in the post-colonial state. He further contends that this strategy predicated upon the colonial policy of economic exploitation of the local area in an instrument used to sustain the self-interest of the ruling classes while the rural communities suffer under poor, hash and stagnated conditions.

Aborisade (2008) in his book highlighted the various development programmes designed by successive governments in Nigeria, which imed at developing the rural communities. He gives an example of River Basin and Rural Development Authorities established in 1975 o promote rural development. He laments that in practice the scheme bloated bureaucracies feeding on mega million-naira contracts for irrigation and other agricultural projects while the rural areas for which they are meant seemed to have recorded deeper in debilitating poverty.

Finally, from the extensive review of literature, it is obvious that scholars like Akpan, (2002), Olisa (2002) and Olowu (2008) regretted that rural development activities and programmes of the past decades of national independence have not transformed the country's rural areas in the modern, well supplied contended that prosperous population envisaged are the beginning of national sovereignty. They concluded that in terms at the number of programmes identification pursued, rural development in Nigeria has made little transformatary impact. They cite basic social services, public utilities and essential infrastructure as still being woefully inadequate in almost all corners of the country.

In Nigeria, past centralized development efforts embarked upon had resulted into failure to benefit the rural people yet; these people cannot be neglected for its enormity. For instance, in Nigeria, the population of people residing in rural areas in few selected states is Rivers 86.16%, Anambra 80:85%, Bauchi 76:8%, Oyo 37:84% Ondo 25.8%, Kano 89:6%, Sokoto 38:7% Kwara 52.0%, Plateau 69:0%, Ogun 68:3% and Adamawa 71:5% (Olojede, 2017). It has therefore been realized that rural development must constitute a major part of a development strategy if a large segment of those in greatest need are to benefit since most programmes embarked upon by the central and state governments have failed in these areas; then local government becomes the next agent to fall on for development.

THESE ARE ROLES OF LOCAL GOVERNMENT IN RURAL DEVELOPMENT:

Education: Local governments through their local education districts have been responsible for the construction, maintenance and staffing of primary schools in their respective areas. Also, it is responsible for the payment of salaries for teaching and non – teaching staff in primary schools.

Transportation: The provision of transportation has gone a long way to enhance the status of Nigerian local governments. These local governments have set up diverse mass urban transit scheme to help to transport their staff and also act as a source of revenue generation for local governments.

Public Toilet: Local governments are not left out in the maintenance of good hygienic culture. They embark on the construction of public toilet for their people.

Water Supply: Local governments embark on digging of bore holes in the rural areas; this has greatly improved the hygiene nature of the people in these rural communities.

Medical and Health: These include the provision, maintenance and administration of dispensaries, maternity and health centres. The increase in the revenue allocation to local governments has been helping in the maintenance of these medical and health services.

Law Enforcement: Customary courts of Grades A, B and C and setup in different local government areas. These courts deal with civil cases such as divorce, defaulters and issuing of certificate of marriage Nehru (2006) emphasized the role of local government as the basis of any true system of democracy. According to him, the role of local government includes the following;

Grass-root democracy: Local government provides scope for democracy at the grass – root level. If direct democracy can still be practicable, it is only at this level, otherwise democracy at the state or national level has become only indirect type.

Serves as a training School: Local government is an excellent ground for creating and training future leaders. The participation of people at the local level in the management of their own affairs, gives them necessary experience to handle bigger affairs later at the state or national level.

Encourages participation of the people in public affairs: Local government affords opportunity to the people to participate in public affairs. It has become impracticable for common people to participate in public affairs at the state or national level.

Reduces the burden of the central government: Local government in a way acts supplementary to the central government. No doubt historically the local government is prior to the state or national government, but with the passage of time many important functions got transferred to the central government.

Serves as a channel of communication: The local government serves as two-way channel of communication between itself and the central government. Desires and aspirations of the local community are articulated and carried upward to the state government, and plans and programmes of the state and the central governments flow in the reverse direction.

Vital for national progress: Local government promotes diversity of experience and creative activity through democratic action. Thus, it contributes to national progress through resilience, strength and richness of democracy.

<u>CONCLUSION</u>

The research looked at the role of Local Government in rural development in Nkanu East Local Government Area, Enugu State within the period 2008-2018.

The study revealed that within the period under review, there was a significant improvement in the provision of basic infrastructure and general poverty in various communities in the state. The general observation made in the state showed that provision of basic infrastructures and other development projects skewed more to the urban areas to the detriment of the rural areas where majority of the population live.

The recognition and importance of local government in the development process is prompted by the imperative to tackle local socio-economic problems and to manage grassroots development through provision of basic rural infrastructure. This research work has demonstrated the weakness of local government in responding to the challenges of rural infrastructure provision and delivery. The rural infrastructure network is unavailable in the local areas and where it is available; it is severely degraded and inadequate for any meaningful development. Based on this, the following suggestions are put forth to enhance the delivery capacity of local government and enable the rural people enjoy the presence of basic rural infrastructure.

Local Government is the focus of government efforts at promoting development. To effectively develop, the people's efforts must be adequately mobilized. A Purposeful combination of local (peoples) efforts and energies with that of government with the objective of improving socioeconomic conditions and encouraging political participation are key factors in rural development.

Rural Development as a strategy is designed to improve the economic and social life of the rural people. The core issues in rural development include self-help; attention to needs (felt and latent); integrated community for development; mobilization of human and material resources which could facilitate the provision of social amenities and infrastructures. The organizational environment for enhancing rural development remains the local government.

<u>RECOMMENDATIONS</u>

Based on the findings, the following recommendations have been made:

. The roles played by the local governments can be said to be very successful. Though, there is need for the government to increase their function capacity of these projects and programmes to be able to cover every area of the state.

. The government should always maintain a balance in development both in urban and rural areas of the state to minimize migration.

. Local governments should be more people-centered in approach, such that necessary collaboration/partnership with communities in its domain can facilitate the process of rural development.

4. The local government as grassroots government is increasingly challenging. Because of this, there is need for the federal allocation to be increased and has to go straight to the local government account to avoid interference by the state government and caretakership system should be stopped, by so

doing, it will go a long way in having more developmental projects.

5. Local government needs to diversify their internal revenue sources by engaging in some business ventures like filling stations, transportation, and so on, to be able to compliment the poor budgetary allocation given to them by the federal and state government.